December Musings

Advent + 1

by
Susan Anderson

Spring View Publications
info@springview.uk

Copyright © Susan Anderson 2023

The right of Susan Anderson to be identified as the author of this work has been asserted by her in accordance with the Copyright, Design and Patents Act 1988

All Scripture quotations are taken from the Holy Bible, New International Version, NIV. Copyright ©1973, 1978, 1984, 2011 by Biblica, Inc. Used by permission of Zondervan. All rights reserved worldwide. www.zondervan.com The "NIV" and "New International Version" are trademarks registered in the United States Patent and Trademark Office by Biblica, Inc.

Cover image from NASA – A Star from the Lizard Constellation Photobombs Hubble Observation

Typeset by Candy Evans, Kenilworth

Printed and bound by IngramSpark
ingramspark.com

ISBN 978-1-7398659-2-4

With thanks to Michael, family, friends
and the magnificent Candy Evans

December 1st – A Faith
Journey 1

December 2nd – Looking for
the Star 2

December 3rd – 7am 4

December 4th – Sky 5

December 5th – Cute 6

December 6th – Christmas
Lights 7

December 7th – A Moment
of Madness 8

December 8th – A Moment
of Kindness 10

December 9th – A Moment
of Sheer Delight 11

December 10th – Tinsel 12

December 11th – Winter
Glitter Ball 13

December 12th – The
Shepherds 14

December 13th – Virgen de
la Esperanza de Macarena de
Sevilla 16

December 14th – My Idea of
Heaven 18

December 15th – Early
Morning Purr 20

December 16th – Snowflakes
  21

December 17th – Garden
Mulling 22

December 18th – Pusscat 23

December 19th – Advent
Door 24

December 20th – Dogs in
Antlers! 26

December 21st – This
Christmas 27

December 22nd – Warm 28

December 23rd – It's All
About the Boy 29

December 24th – Christmas
Eve and Tomorrow 30

January 6th – Epiphany 32

December 1st – A Faith Journey

The next step can seem as wide as the galaxies,

As deep as the oceans, as invisible as the air we breathe.

Looking for answers, looking for anything some days

We lose sight of the light, lose sight of ourselves.

But God is with us, he sees our weary ways,

And His words envelop us, like a throw

On a cold winter's day,

Warmth reaches our bones, our very souls.

And, as the heat of His word rises

So do we, the next step on the faith journey

Reveals itself, tiny steps for some,

A whole road map for others.

Wherever the journey takes us

God's love leads and guides.

And, we need not be afraid of

What awaits around a blind corner.

Jesus is there, waiting to take our hand

And we can be ready to leave footprints

Of faith for others to see.

December 2nd – Looking for the Star

From the dark

A light shimmers.

Heavy energy burns boldly,

Getting brighter, potent, such electricity,

Sparkles catch the eyes,

And hearts miss a beat.

We choose our star,

That one,

My celestial, my hope,

My little piece of sky.

The glitter ball moves across the deep black of night,

Not yet in the right place

But it knows where it needs to be

At the right moment, on a special day.

Cosmology co-ordinates fixed

The star keeps moving.

Faster, faster
Time ticks away
Close now, the time is near.
Advent's clock counts down.
The star marks and marks
Getting nearer, just that bit closer.
The light burns brighter,
Hearts open wider,
Eyes soften.
The star sends her beautiful tender beam
And settles softly on the sleeping babe.
Bathed in God's light, He sleeps.
The star is done,
Now we must shine and lead the way.

December 3rd – 7am

Rooftops poke above the white blanket,
Trees stolen by stealth coverings.
Helios yet to make his presence felt.
Pale light casts no shadow,
It's a world end silence,
As I peer out across the ancient tops
Of old town houses, chimney pots
Defy the grasping grey mists.
Pink shades tinge the horizon,
Dawn's lipstick slicked across early skies.
Sunlight burns through, clean blue appears
And the clinging cover scurries, melts away.
Blackbirds scuttle across the icing sugar lawn,
The day has started, kettle on!

December 4th – Sky

Pentland Hills hidden by grey blanket clouds,

Rain as sharp as glass shards fall on windows.

Looking out, it's a waiting game,

A lull to brave Mother Nature's full flight weather bomb,

She's wielded wild skies,

She's shouting,

She's at full tilt,

She's saying, "Just remember who you are!"

December 5th – Cute

The puppy next door,
What a delight, such love in a small
Bundle of soft paws.

December 6th – Christmas Lights

Christmas lights adorn towns, houses, even garden gnomes,

Children stop and stare at Rudolph, Santa and

All kinds of snowmen. Are there always more?

It seems so, the winter tribe

And penguins add to the show.

New families appear on lawns,

A true melting pot

And they all get along!

As the lights twinkle and glow

Perhaps they bring a little smile

And on dark December nights.

December 7th – A Moment of Madness

When I woke up, I thought that's it
I'll invade, blackbird's saying no
But I ain't listening.
You see I think I'm afraid,
Unloved, ugly, misguided, deluded
All the rubbish synaptic rubbish I eat every day.
The bitterness burns and sours
Everything, all the apocalyptic menu on my plate.
No toasted marshmallows around the fire
With friends to sweeten the end of my day.
So I go to bed, sleep beckons
My invasions plans fill the dark looming void.
And a voices instructs,
I have to do it,
I have to do it.
It's for the best,
It's for the best.

As I cry out for the right thing to do
It goes unheard, a deafness
And all I can see is winning,
It seems worth more than a baby's smile,
A child's delight at holding mum's hand,
More than silent skies and silent sleep,
And waking to hear a blackbird sing.
But madness has a grip on me,
And in a moment I had woken
And thought I'll invade
I've got nothing better to do today!

December 8th – A Moment of Kindness

Forever should be filled kindness,
Just kindness, no puppet strings attached.
But, instead grown-ups still see
Life as a soap opera playground continuation.
Name calling, girls brawling and pulling hair,
Pushing and shoving, fingers in backs,
And worst of all not allowing someone in the gang.
The everyday petulance falls into a black hole
Welcomes and embraces the adults who
Should know better, should just be better.
Legacy's a big word, bloody big capitals required,
Just sayin'
But kindness is in life's T's and C's
Do read your small print,
We would like a better world,
Is it too much to ask?

December 9th – A Moment of Sheer Delight

And as the belly grows and grows,
A flicker of movement,
Brings a smile.
The babe inside pushes
And stretches the cocoon home.
It's a moment of delight.

The winter dead vistas are filled
With a forget-me-not blue haze.
Spring runs amok, neon greens appear,
Brash bold yellow daffodils strut their stuff
Wild garlic carpets the soil, sentry red tulips line up,
It's a moment of delight.

December 10th – Tinsel

Tinsel wraps around trees, dogs, babes,

Happy families come out to play, it's all a bit crackers but oh so much fun,

In dark winter nights footprints arrive on cotton white lawns,

Red Robin has waited for his turn in the yuletide spotlight,

Decking the halls, holly is everywhere, gloss green leaves, ruby berries,

Down time, rush time, list time, mustn't forgot a thing time!

Early dawns, crystal bright, frost drips cling to stubborn rose buds,

Cold winds whistle across barren, bleak lands,

Early morning, a weak sun, winter solstice to come,

Mince pies, warm pastry promises of heady spice aromas,

Bracelets of lights drape from winter-bare trees,

Each Advent window opens, sweet or not!

Reaching for hope might just be the best present of all.

December 11th – Winter Glitter Ball

Strictly delights on Saturday nights,
Floating ball gowns, fleet of foot
Dancing, amazing impossible lifts,
Sequins, lace, spray tans
And glimpses of Peaty's pecs.
Lithe limbs, liquid lines, Anton quips
And Craig's disdain, too many nines
But every now and again he melts,
It's a ten!
A tango to take your breath away,
Too sexy but you'll watch
And wish it was you.
A waltz as light as candy floss,
Timeless elegance, timeless grace.
Music to fill your soul, feet cannot resist
Tapping a jive beat, fingers click
To a hot sizzling samba.
In a blink it's time to vote,
Heart and head go into battle,
And in a flash, it's cast.
This world away fairground
Affords a little escape on a carousel
Of joy and too much of everything.

December 12th – The Shepherds

As sure as the sun sets,
Well beaten paths and places to rest
Are found in these eternal pastures,
But something heavenly happened here long ago.
Sheep stood rooted to the ground, shepherds watched
Over the flock, all counted, all safe and sound.
The clear starlit sky, nothing new, usual view,
But this night, this night was like no other,
A glance up from the flock and before them
An angel descended, a light like no other.
Fear gripped them then Gabriel spoke,
This was news like no other,
"Do not be afraid. I bring you good news
Of great joy that will be for all people."   *Luke 2:10-11*
And the host of angels appeared,
A gathering like no other.
Heaven bound the angels ascended
And suddenly the shepherds were alone,
Bethlehem beckoned, a Saviour to see,
A sign, a gift like no other.

And today those fields remain unchanged,
The sun still sets over these unremarkable pastures.
As I sit and look to where shepherds once sat,
I see them, I see the sheep, I hear the words,
"Glory to God in the highest,
and on earth peace to men on
whom his favour rests." *Luke 2:14*
This is a story like no other, this is a story like no other!

December 13th – Virgen de la Esperanza de Macarena de Sevilla

She carries hope, she is carried,

Candlelit, glowing in the darkness,

Streets bear witness

To the passing by of hope,

A chance for thankfulness

And a chance to pray.

This is their faith, not mine nor yours

Perhaps, but these are fine margins

And belief is a personal thing.

Strength carries her through narrow streets,

Men weighed down by heavy decoration,

The bejewelled opulent canopy overcomes,

Each step taken brings pain,

Shoulders have to take the strain

But, still they carry her.

As the night sees the procession come to a close

Hope returns to her basilica home,
She is set down, she can rest.
And, things were thought,
Things were said, prayers made,
Things to hope for, a love to share.
And on this planet, this vast home,
A new dawn will herald processions
Of all faiths, each a personal thing.
Whatever offers hope in our daily lives
Let's simply embrace.

December 14th – My Idea of Heaven

with thanks to the Revd Dawn Saunders

Listening to words from the heart,
Refines, re-configures my perspective
On what matters, and I dive into
What heaven can be.
It isn't fixed, it's a fluidity,
A feeling of belonging,
A place you can just be,
A place of welcome, no judgement,
Come on in, we all fit in.
It isn't about things and stuff,
Life's jewellery, bought and worn once
It's having family gems, free purchase,
Free from cost, just refractions,
With the odd inclusion.
You shine some days,
But days when lustre deserts,
Someone puts you on their finger.

The heaven ring glows and restores.
It isn't place, a sun drenched
Bleached white beach,
It isn't fancies, but now
And then a necessary vice.
It's being with someone to share
The day, the night, the dawn
And as the sun sets, heaven could just be
An evening at Café Morso.
Heaven is home where no one
Is a stranger.

December 15th – Early Morning Purr

My lioness wakes me,
Her inner purring motor soothes,
Gentle fine grain sandpaper licks
Tell me breakfast is requested.
My lioness then nips and bites,
I lie still, hoping this feline will
Stop and settle by my feet,
She won't, I should know better!
My lioness gets her way,
We both head to the kitchen,
Behind the cupboard door
Lies Sheba treasure and more.
My lioness flits through the cat flap,
And she's away to prowl,
Glorious stealth, a lethal languid lynx.
My lioness will return just as
My tea is sip perfect,
She'll join me, nudging the mug,
Demanding fuss and favour, such a queen.
But my lioness, in these early hours
My cup of tea is sacrosanct
And Pepsi, you'll just have to wait!

December 16th – Snowflakes

Each floating, drifting, dawdling flake
Falls through the air.
Each a mystery, a different shape
No two the same.
And as we wonder about our little
Home, the building blocks of the universe
Are locked into these marvels of nature.
Ice branches, symmetry of such exquisite frozen lace.
There's a silent power in the variety,
And as snow layers grow, our feet
Innocently crush white stuff,
All that evolution,
All that chemistry
All that time
Captured in molecules.
And when we're long gone
Please keep falling snowflakes.
We think we're mighty
But each falling mystery flake
Will melt without a second thought about us.

December 17th – Garden Mulling

Over the fence the gardener and I chatted,
About this and that, memories from
Childhood, snowy days, doing the Christmas post days.
Grandfather butchers, making sausages,
Not touching the bacon slicer!
Football teams and he's a red,
George Best and Johan Cruyff,
Forgot to mention Eric,
Sorry Monsieur Cantona, another day perhaps.
Global warming, roses still in bloom,
The mint is growing, lady's mantle
Is doing her thing.
As the tree gets its haircut
And I plant forgotten bulbs,
Great Morley's words ring in my ears.
Time in the garden, is time to forget life's white noise
And lose yourself in Mother Nature.
He was right, I felt lighter.

December 18th – Pusscat

Cat says hello,
I say hello,
Knitted together with purring
Stitches, we sit together and ponder.
I think of lists,
Cat thinks of mice.
Serenity, soft fur, silky paws
Make for a few minutes of calm.
Cat jumps down,
I get up.
Same time, same place tomorrow.

December 19th – Advent Door

Saturday morning slumber, slow start,
Advent calendar opened, an angel
HALLELUJAH!
I say hello, this messenger has been
Waiting a long time, she's here now.
Thoughts turn to the Child
And on a table in the hall,
Lies Jesus, in manger, Nativity central,
Full cast, ready to go!
Scene set, night time candles cast a glow,
A curtain rises for mankind
And the light is the same, year on year.
Do I hear a whisper as I pass by?
Perhaps I need to stop and listen
Just a little more.

Ridiculous lists are made, some seem endless,
Some even pointless but, they beckon as the
Sun sets on such plans bravely made,
Tomorrow's dawn and mists crowd the sky,
Visitors soon, must get ready, a table to set.
Out of practice, timings slip and slide,
Smiles as champagne bubbles surf the brain
And kitchen chaos reigns supreme.
Visitors are replete, time to leave,
And we head towards the door
A glance to the right and we speak
Of the Child, if I listen hard enough
If I listen hard enough...

December 20th – Dogs in Antlers!

And so the Christmas adverts roll out,
Perfumes, pixies and perfect presents,
Fairies, light up jumpers, canapes of every flavour,
For every occasion, catering on a galactic scale.
And chocolate orange panettone who knew?
The must have, the latest thing,
Traditions changing, disappearing,
More of everything.
But, they say it's being together that counts.
Candles, twinkling lights, starry skies
Shine out from black screens.
Starring roles for Santa,
Always upstaged by Rudolph
And his flying friends.
But, as hard as I look,
Not a wise man in sight!

December 21st – This Christmas

Nativity flexes her muscles,
Now is the time, places found
To set the figures down,
A baby looks out,
A million faces stare in.
As we gaze, we can begin again,
The face of Jesus telling us,
God's peace is here for all.

Mary placed here, Joseph there.
The Magi, star led,
Shepherds, angel called.
And this humble manger scene
Has strength beyond the window,
Beyond the shelf, beyond the mantelpiece.
When all is packed away, the story stays alive,
God's love is here for all.

December 22nd – Warm

Bitter cold seeps into your soul,

The wind sharp enough to make

Cuts through the warmest of coats.

Standing on a doorstep to

Say hello, just a few minutes I'll be

But, in the winter chill thirty

Minutes fly by, chat will do that

And I felt warm,

Friendship will do that.

December 23rd – It's All About the Boy

The calendar marks our Advent time,
Another window opens
Time flies,
Reflections of the year flicker by.

Each picture, a Christmas pointer,
Full of hope, expectation,
Lead us towards a place
of reconciliation.

It's all about the promise,
It's all about peace
It's all about love for one another
It's all about grace
It's all about the boy
In a manger.

December 24th – Christmas Eve and Tomorrow

Boxes of delight are under the tree,
Candles glow, flames flicker,
Elegant towers of light.
Carols ring out, reach out
From radios, TV screens,
Hubs and each other.
Choristers from Kings
Sing, filling the house,
With a warm wave
Of all things certain.

And as we sit, firework primed,
We reflect before the
Blue touch papers are lit.
A year of such extremes,
Too hard to write them all,
But we have felt every twist
And turn of this roller coaster ride.
And have we screamed!

And as the babe in a manger,
Looks out, the journey begins again
For us, ambitions will run amok.
Dreams, ideas, no full stops.
Being the best we can be
Topping the list?
We will fail at times, not every day a success,
Trying is good enough, hold on to that.
Bethlehem seems far away,
But it's here in your homes
For today and tomorrow.

January 6th – Epiphany

A journey like no other,
We know them as Magi,
Nativity introductions, antique names,
What value today?
Their jewelled silk garbs fluttered in the breeze,
Against the ink blue night cool desert skies
As diamond stud stars mapped the way.
As camels crossed the sandy seas
Did their regal passengers question, did they dread?
What conversations passed their lips?
What to believe?
What will we see?
Will it be golden and glittering?
Will we know it is he?
At the lowly manger they knelt
Before the babe of love and hope.

No fanfare, no peeling of bells, no Las Vegas side show.

The shepherds came despite their fear.

Together they believed

So why don't we?

To turn back time,

To be in that stable,

To make the journey,

To see the angels.

What would we have said?

And as those camels turned for the journey home

Did the Magi ask themselves, "Was that really the Son of God?"

www.ingramcontent.com/pod-product-compliance
Lightning Source LLC
Chambersburg PA
CBHW071325080526
44587CB00018B/3350